BOOK CODE

R772000

AV² **by Weigl** brings you media enhanced books that support active learning.

AV² provides enriched content that supplements and complements this book. Weigl's AV² books strive to create inspired learning and engage young minds for a total learning experience.

Go to **www.av2books.com**, and enter this book's unique code. You will have access to video, audio, web links, quizzes, a slide show, and activities.

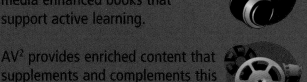

Audio
Listen to sections of the book read aloud.

Video
Watch informative video clips.

Web Link
Find research sites and play interactive games.

Try This!
Complete activities and hands-on experiments.

Due to the dynamic nature of the Internet, some of the URLs and activities provided as part of AV² by Weigl may have changed or ceased to exist. AV² by Weigl accepts no responsibility for any such changes. All media enhanced books are regularly monitored to update addresses and sites in a timely manner. Contact AV² by Weigl at 1-866-649-3445 or av2books@weigl.com with any questions, comments, or feedback.

Published by AV² by Weigl
350 5ᵗʰ Avenue, 59ᵗʰ Floor
New York, NY 10118
www.av2books.com   www.weigl.com

Library of Congress Cataloging-in-Publication Data available upon request.
Fax 1-866-44-WEIGL for the attention of the Publishing Records department.

ISBN 978-1-61690-154-7 (hard cover)
ISBN 978-1-61690-155-4 (soft cover)

Printed in the United States of America in North Mankato, Minnesota
1 2 3 4 5 6 7 8 9 0 14 13 12 11 10

052010
WEP264000

Editor: Heather C. Hudak
Design: Terry Paulhus

Photograph Credits
Weigl acknowledges Getty Images as the primary image supplier for this title.

Every reasonable effort has been made to trace ownership and to obtain permission to reprint copyright material. The publishers would be pleased to have any errors or omissions brought to their attention so that they may be corrected in subsequent printings.

Contents

Who Is Robert Pattinson?. 4

Growing Up 6

Practice Makes Perfect 8

Key Events 10

What Is an Actor? 12

Influences. 14

Overcoming Obstacles 16

Achievements and Successes 18

Write a Biography 20

Timeline. 22

Words to Know/Index 23

Log on to www.av2books.com. 24

Who Is Robert Pattinson?

Playing Edward Cullen in the Twilight movies has made Robert Pattinson one of the most popular actors today. Robert began his professional acting career in 2004, and after just a few years, he has become a well-known actor. Thanks to his performances in the Twilight movies, Robert has been nominated for and won many awards, including the 2009 MTV Movie Award for Best Male Breakthrough Performance.

In addition to acting, Robert plays guitar and piano. When he is not on a film set, Robert enjoys writing and performing music. He also likes spending time with friends and family at his home in London, England.

"Nothing, I don't think, can prepare you for the fans. I don't know why I'm not getting used to it, but I'm completely overwhelmed every time."

Growing Up

Robert Thomas Pattinson was born on May 13, 1986, in London, England. He grew up in the suburb of Barnes, about 7 miles (11 kilometers) southwest of London. Robert's father, Richard, sold classic cars that he **imported** from the United States. Robert's mother, Clare, worked for a modeling agency.

Robert has two older sisters, Elizabeth and Victoria. Victoria works for an ad agency. Elizabeth, or Lizzy, is a songwriter and singer.

Growing up, Robert loved music. He began playing the piano at age three and the guitar at five. Robert liked to entertain his family. When he was not making music, Robert enjoyed watching cartoons. *Sharky & George* and *Hammerman*, which starred rapper MC Hammer, were his favorite cartoons.

■ Robert wanted to become a writer before he started his acting career.

Get to Know London, England

TREE
OAK

FLAG

FLOWER
RED ROSE

Atlantic Ocean

North Sea

IRELAND

| 0 | 200 Miles |
| 0 | 200 Kilometers |

London is the capital of the United Kingdom. The United Kingdom is made up of England, Scotland, Wales, and Northern Ireland.

London is located on the banks of the Thames River, in southeast England.

The British Royal family lives in Buckingham Palace while they are in London.

The London Eye is the largest Ferris wheel in Europe. It can carry 800 passengers at a time.

The Crown Jewels are kept at the Tower of London.

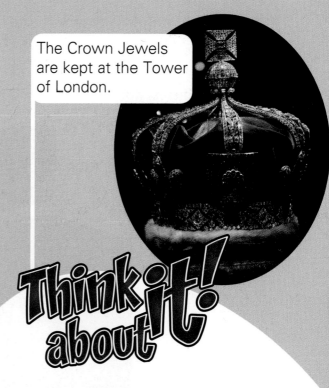

Think about it!

Robert was encouraged to study music and drama as a child. He starred in school productions and learned to play instruments at a young age. What special skills or hobbies are important to your family? Do your friends share any of these skills? In what ways can you put these skills to use?

Practice Makes Perfect

Robert attended Tower House School, an all-boys private school. He was known as the student with the messiest desk. Robert enjoyed drama class. He was in school productions from the age of six.

As a teenager, Robert began attending Harrodian School. This school is known for its drama program, called the Barnes Theatre Club. Robert's first play with the club was *Guys and Dolls*. He appeared as a Cuban dancer. Later, he landed the lead role in *Tess of the D'Urbervilles*. An **agent** soon recognized his talent.

■ In 2010, Robert was listed by *Time Magazine* as one of the most influential people.

With the agent's help, Robert began landing professional acting roles. At the age of 17, Robert was cast in the TV movie *The Ring of Nibelungs*. In 2004, Robert won his first movie role. He worked with Reese Witherspoon and Gabriel Byrne in *Vanity Fair*.

The following year, Robert won the role of Cedric Diggory in *Harry Potter and the Goblet of Fire*. After a year-long break from acting, Robert appeared in a string of **independent** movies, including *The Haunted Airman*, *The Bad Mother's Handbook*, *The Summer House*, *How To Be*, and *Little Ashes*. Although he was working as an actor, Robert was not sure he wanted to make acting a full-time career.

■ Robert filmed *Harry Potter and the Goblet of Fire* for 11 months. During that time, he became friends with many of the cast members.

Key Events

Robert received a great deal of attention for his performance as Cedric Diggory in *Harry Potter and the Goblet of Fire*. He was called the next Jude Law by *Teen People* magazine. Instead of appearing in major motion pictures, Robert took roles in low-budget films. These films did not make an impact at the **box office**, but they showed Robert's acting range.

In 2007, Robert flew to Venice, California, to **audition** for *Twilight* director Catherine Hardwicke. Kristen Stewart had already been cast as the female lead, Bella Swan. Kristen and Robert read **lines** together for Catherine. After, Kristen told Catherine that she thought Rob was the perfect actor to play Edward Cullen.

When *Twilight* was released in 2008, it was a huge success. Its opening weekend was one of the most successful of any independent film in history. The *Twilight* movie soundtrack debuted at number one on the **Billboard** albums chart. Robert sings two songs on the soundtrack, "Let Me Sign" and "Never Think."

The following year, Robert starred in the *Twilight* sequel, *New Moon*. This movie was even more successful than the first.

■ Robert was picked from 3,000 actors to play the lead role of teen vampire Edward Cullen.

Thoughts from Robert

In television and magazine interviews, Robert often shares his thoughts about his experience playing Edward Cullen. He also talks about stardom and playing music.

Robert talks about playing Edward Cullen.

"I spent a long time trying to figure out how to play [Edward's part] without making a fool out of myself. The whole book is written from Bella's perspective and she's in love with him."

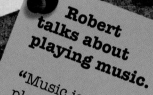

Robert talks about playing music.

"Music is my back-up plan if acting fails. I don't want to put all my eggs in one basket."

Robert talks about how he prepared for _Twilight_.

"I was alone for a very long time. I went to Oregon before anyone else, about two and a half months before, and just didn't talk to anyone. I worked with a trainer every day and went running, but I tried not to speak to anyone."

Robert talks about his life.

"I'm happy with the life I have now. I've got the same two friends I've had since I was 12, and I can't see that changing."

Robert talks about the music he wrote for _Twilight_.

"I did a scene where I played a thing that I made up. It was the best piano piece I've ever done in my life, but it didn't really fit. In the end, as part of the whole score, it is very different than what I came up with."

Robert talks about how he relates to Edward Cullen.

"Stubbornness in some ways about some things. He's pretty self-righteous. I guess I could get possessive about certain things, obsessive as well, I think."

What Is an Actor?

Actors are people who pretend to be other people in theater, radio, television, and movie productions. Most actors train at special schools or work with a drama coach to improve their acting skills. To make a character more realistic, some actors draw on other skills, such as dancing and singing.

Often, actors must learn lines and movements that are written in scripts. Sometimes, actors do not use a script. They say and do what they feel in the moment. This is called improvisation. Some actors, such as Robert, gain experience through theatrical productions.

■ Robert had not read the Twilight series of books before auditioning for the part of Edward Cullen.

Actors 101

Dakota Fanning (1994–)

Dakota was born in Conyers, Georgia. As a child, she performed in local theater productions. Dakota's first big acting break came when she was cast in the movie *I am Sam* with Sean Penn and Michelle Pfeiffer. She was **nominated** for a Screen Actors Guild Award for her work in this movie. At the age of eight, Dakota was the youngest person ever nominated for this award. In 2009, Dakota was cast as Jane in *New Moon*.

Daniel Radcliffe (1989–)

Daniel was born in Fulham, England. In 1999, he landed his first professional acting role in the television movie *David Copperfield*. Two years later, Daniel was cast as Harry Potter in the movie *Harry Potter and the Sorcerer's Stone*. In 2010, he was nominated for a People's Choice Award for Favorite On-screen Team, alongside cast mates Rupert Grint and Emma Watson.

Michael Cera (1988–)

Michael was born in Brampton, Ontario, Canada. He has been nominated for many awards, including the MTV Movie Award for Best Male Performance for his role in *Juno*. In 2009, Michael ranked number one on *Entertainment Weekly*'s "30 Under 30" actors list. His first breakthrough role was on the television series *Arrested Development*.

Vanessa Hudgens (1988–)

Vanessa was born in Salinas, California. She is an actor, dancer, and singer. Vanessa is best known for portraying Gabriella Montez in the *High School Musical* movies. She released her first solo album, *V*, in 2006. It debuted at number 24 on the U.S. Billboard album chart. In 2009, Vanessa won Favorite Movie Actress at the Kids' Choice Awards.

Scripts

Scripts are written documents that contain the lines and movements for movie roles. When preparing for a role, actors receive a script. They memorize the lines their character speaks and the actions they must make with their body. Scripts also provide stage directions and suggestions for how the set should look.

Influences

From a young age, Robert's father, Richard, believed his son was a talented actor. He supported Robert's choice to attend Harrodian School so that he could join the theater club. At first, Robert was happy to work backstage. Then, his father encouraged Robert to try out for parts in plays.

Robert was 13 years old when he discovered the works of award-winning actor Jack Nicholson. Jack was born in 1937 in New Jersey and is known for his portrayals of dark, unusual characters. He has been nominated 12 times for an Academy Award. This is considered the most respected acting award. Jack has won the award twice for Best Actor and once for Best Supporting Actor.

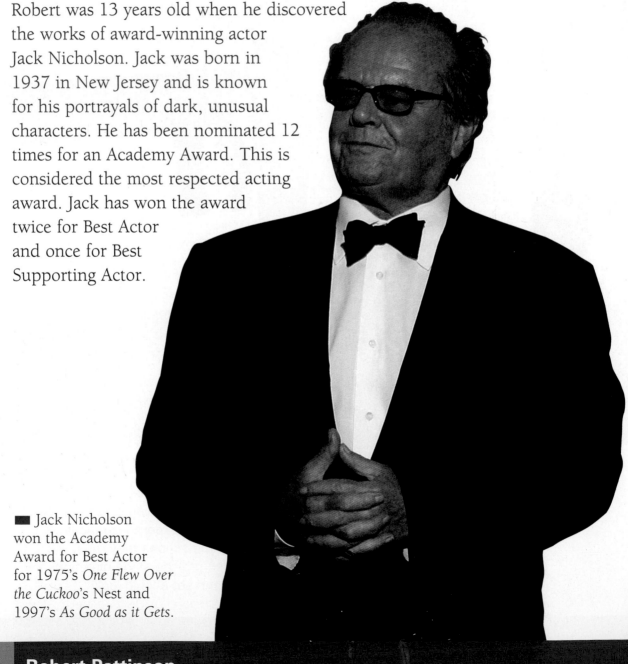

■ Jack Nicholson won the Academy Award for Best Actor for 1975's *One Flew Over the Cuckoo's Nest* and 1997's *As Good as it Gets*.

Jack became Robert's favorite actor. Robert tried copying Jack's gestures and his accent. When Robert began acting professionally, he considered how Jack would portray the same characters. Like Jack, Robert was drawn to unusual characters.

TWILIGHT FAMILY

In the Twilight movies, Edward Cullen and Jacob Black, Taylor Lautner's character, are not friends. Both men want the affection of Bella Swan, played by Kristen Stewart. Despite their on-screen **rivalry**, Robert is friends with Taylor. Robert is also close with other Twilight saga stars, such as Kristen Stewart and Nikki Reed. They often are seen eating at restaurants or taking part in other activities together after work.

Kristen, Taylor, and Robert often attend events together to help promote the Twilight movies. In 2009, they attended the San Diego Comic-Con, a comic convention.

Overcoming Obstacles

Robert began his acting career while he was still in school. He was very busy and found it challenging to work and study at the same time. Robert worked hard to find a balance between completing schoolwork while modeling, auditioning, and acting in theater productions.

Robert's performance in the TV movie *The Ring of the Nibelungs* caught the attention of *Vanity Fair* director Mira Nair. She gave Robert a small part in *Vanity Fair*, but his scenes were cut. Robert was then hired for the 2005 UK Royal Court Theatre premiere of *The Woman Before*. However, he was replaced by another actor. Robert did not give up on his dream of becoming an actor. He kept auditioning for roles.

■ When it was first announced that Robert would be playing the role of Edward Cullen, he received bags of letters from people who thought he was not the right person for the part.

Many of the *Harry Potter and the Goblet of Fire* cast members had bonded during previous films. Robert was new to the cast, and he worked hard to earn the others' respect as an actor and become their friend. After the movie was released, *Screen International* magazine called Robert a "British Star of Tomorrow." However, several years passed before Robert was given the chance to star in another big-budget movie.

When Robert was cast as Edward Cullen, many people were unhappy. Fans of the *Twilight* book did not want an unknown actor to play Edward. More than 75,000 people signed a petition to have Robert removed from the role. Once the movie was released, Robert became an international star. Now, Robert is thankful for his many fans, but he often finds the attention overwhelming.

■ Robert is known for his tousled hairstyle. He tugs at his hair when he is feeling stressed. This makes it look messy.

Achievements and Successes

Although Robert's acting career has just begun, he has already achieved success. His performance as Art in *How To Be* earned Robert the Best Actor award at the Strasbourg Film Festival in 2008. Since then, he has earned many more awards.

Robert received the Hollywood Film Festival's New Hollywood award in 2008. That same year, he was named Yahoo's Top Movie Heartthrob, *Rolling Stone Magazine*'s Hottest Actor, and *Entertainment Tonight*'s Top Hunk. Robert was ranked 23 on Moviefone's "The 25 Hottest Actors Under 25."

■ In addition to his 2009 Teen Choice Award, Robert has been honored for his style. Robert was *GQ Magazine*'s Best Dressed Man of 2010. They called his style elegant and inspiring.

In 2009, Robert won the MTV Movie Award for Best Kiss, which he shared with Kristen Stewart. At the same awards, he won Breakthrough Performance Male for his role as Edward Cullen. Robert then won four Teen Choice awards for his part in *Twilight*.

In 2010, Robert won the People's Choice Award for Favorite On-Screen Team, along with his *New Moon* co-stars Taylor Lautner and Kristen Stewart. He was also nominated in the Favorite Movie Actor category.

Since *Twilight* was released in November 2008, it has earned about $400 million dollars at the box office. Thanks to his part in the success of this movie, Robert has been cast in many more movies, such as *Unbound Captives* and *Bel Ami*.

HELPING OTHERS

Often, actors use their popularity to increase public awareness. They may bring attention to nonprofit organizations, environmental causes, or help fund special causes. Robert lends his support to many charitable organizations, such as the American Foundation for **AIDS** Research. In 2009, two kisses with Robert were auctioned for more than $20,000 each at the annual Cinema Against AIDS gala for the American Foundation for Aids Research. Bidding started at $10,000. To learn more about American Foundation for Aids Research, visit **www.amfar.org**.

Write a Biography

A person's life story can be the subject of a book. This kind of book is called a biography. Biographies describe the lives of remarkable people, such as those who have achieved great success or have done important things to help others. These people may be alive today, or they may have lived many years ago. Reading a biography can help you learn more about a remarkable person.

At school you might be asked to write a biography. First, decide whom you want to write about. You can choose an actor, such as Robert Pattinson, or any other person you find interesting. Then, find out if your library has any books about this person.

Learn as much as you can about him or her. Write down the key events in the person's life. What was this person's childhood like? What has he or she accomplished? What are his or her goals? What makes this person special or unusual?

A concept web is a useful research tool. Read the questions in the following concept web. Answer the questions in your notebook. Your answers will help you write your biography.

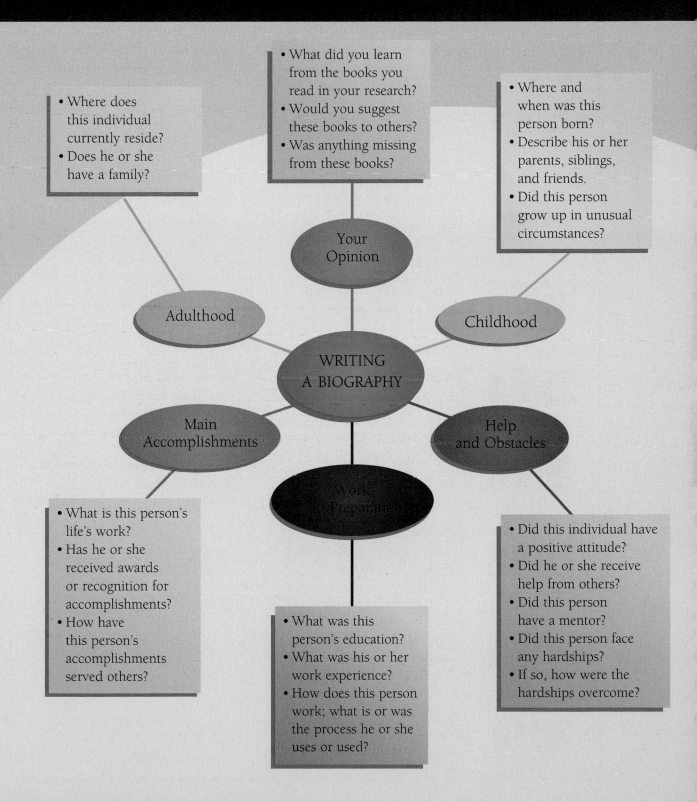

- Where does this individual currently reside?
- Does he or she have a family?

- What did you learn from the books you read in your research?
- Would you suggest these books to others?
- Was anything missing from these books?

- Where and when was this person born?
- Describe his or her parents, siblings, and friends.
- Did this person grow up in unusual circumstances?

Your Opinion

Adulthood

Childhood

WRITING A BIOGRAPHY

Main Accomplishments

Help and Obstacles

Work and Preparation

- What is this person's life's work?
- Has he or she received awards or recognition for accomplishments?
- How have this person's accomplishments served others?

- What was this person's education?
- What was his or her work experience?
- How does this person work; what is or was the process he or she uses or used?

- Did this individual have a positive attitude?
- Did he or she receive help from others?
- Did this person have a mentor?
- Did this person face any hardships?
- If so, how were the hardships overcome?

Timeline

YEAR	ROBERT PATTINSON	WORLD EVENTS
1986	Robert Thomas Pattinson is born.	The Disney channel begins 24-hour service.
2001	Robert joins the Barnes Theatre Club in London.	*Gladiator* wins the Academy Award for Best Picture.
2003	Robert appears in his first TV role in *Ring of the Nibelungs*.	*Spirited Away* wins the Academy Award for Best Animated Feature.
2004	Robert lands his first movie role in *Vanity Fair*.	*Harry Potter and the Prisoner of Azkaban* is released.
2005	Robert plays the role of Cedric Diggory in *Harry Potter and the Goblet of Fire*.	Hilary Swank wins the Academy Award for Best Actress.
2008	Robert appears as Edward Cullen in the film *Twilight*.	*Kung Fu Panda* is released.
2009	Robert returns to his role as Edward Cullen in *New Moon*.	*The Simpsons* begins season 20.
2010	Robert plays Edward Cullen in the third movie of the Twilight Saga, *Eclipse*.	Sandra Bullock wins the Academy Award for Best Actress.

Words to Know

agent: a person who handles business matters for an actor

AIDS: Acquired Immune Deficiency Syndrome; a disease that destroys the body's ability to fight illness

audition: perform to try to get a job in the entertainment industry

Billboard: charts produced by a weekly magazine that rate the popularity of music

box office: the amount of money earned by a movie through sales; the number of people who pay to see a movie in the cinema

imported: brought goods into a country from another country

independent: movies that are not funded by a major studio; they often have a smaller production budget

lines: the words spoken by an actor for a particular role

nominated: added to a list of people who will be considered for awards

rivalry: competition for the same achievement

Index

Cera, Michael 13

Fanning, Dakota 13

Harry Potter 9, 10, 13, 17, 22

Hudgens, Vanessa 13

Lautner, Taylor 15, 19

music 4, 6, 7, 11

Nicholson, Jack 14, 15

Radcliffe, Daniel 13

Stewart, Kristen 10, 15, 19

theater 8, 12, 14, 22

Twilight 4, 10, 11, 15, 17, 19, 22

Log on to www.av2books.com

AV² by Weigl brings you media enhanced books that support active learning. Go to **www.av2books.com**, and enter the special code inside the front cover of this book. You will gain access to enriched and enhanced content that supplements and complements this book. Content includes video, audio, web links, quizzes, a slide show, and activities.

Audio
Listen to sections of the book read aloud.

Video
Watch informative video clips.

Web Link
Find research sites and play interactive games.

Try This!
Complete activities and hands-on experiments.

WHAT'S ONLINE?

Try This! Complete activities and hands-on experiments.	**Web Link** Find research sites and play interactive games.	**Video** Watch informative video clips.	**EXTRA FEATURES**
Pages 6-7 Complete an activity about your childhood.	**Pages 8-9** Learn more about Robert Pattinson's life.	**Pages 4-5** Watch a video about Robert Pattinson.	**Audio** Hear introductory audio at the top of every page.
Pages 10-11 Try this activity about key events.	**Pages 14-15** Find out more about the people who influenced Robert Pattinson.	**Pages 12-13** Check out a video about Robert Pattinson.	**Key Words** Study vocabulary, and play a matching word game.
Pages 16-17 Complete an activity about overcoming obstacles.	**Pages 18-19** Learn more about Robert Pattinson's achievements.		**Slide Show** View images and captions, and try a writing activity.
Pages 20-21 Write a biography.	**Pages 20-21** Check out this site about Robert Pattinson.		**AV² Quiz** Take this quiz to test your knowledge
Page 22 Try this timeline activity.			